Dear Parent:

You and your child are about to embark on an extraordinary adventure in learning!

Hi, we're Mom and Dad Rymon. Welcome to our home! Come visit with our wonderfully, zany family and friends and we'll develop your child's imagination and thinking skills.

Like all of the delightful Rhyme Time with the Rymons products, our story, Wakin' to the Bacon, is much more than entertainment. The storybook, audiotape, and additional activities are based on a realistic family experience. Together, they form a true learning experience that lets your child practice the reasoning and problem-solving skills so crucial for school success.

The Thinking Well people have carefully woven thinking questions throughout our story and audiotape. Discover how these simple, yet mind-stretching questions enrich the story, stimulate discussion, and inspire your child to ask even more questions. And our story especially helps your child to imagine, to practice decision-making, and to evaulate.

Now, sit back with your child and enjoy! It's Rhyme Time with the Rymons!

Thoughtfully yours,

Mom and Dad
Rymon

Chuckleberry

ZZZ

ISBN 1-55999-137-2

A division of LinguiSystems, Inc.

Thinking Well
3100 4th Avenue
East Moline, IL 61244

1-800-U-2-THINK

Rhyme Time with the Rymons
Wakin' to the Bacon

Story by Susan Rose Simms
Illustrated by Paul Dallgas-Frey

One bright sunny day, in a house much like yours,
The Rymons were up and beginning their chores.
Eric, the oldest, was feeding the pup,
While eight year old Brent got the table set up.

Dark haired Emily, who just had turned six,
Was pouring the milk while Mom stirred pancake mix.
Dad had the eggs frying up in the pan,
And everything worked out according to plan.

What other kitchen jobs have to be done before the Rymons can eat breakfast?

But it hadn't always been going this way.
So, let's take a look at them just yesterday.

Dad awoke, gave his clock a light tap,
Then settled back down for a 5 minute nap.

When all of a sudden, he felt something wet—
The nose and rough tongue of his droopy-eyed pet.
"Oh, no, Chuckleberry," he said to his pup.
"I can't ignore YOU when it's time to get up!"

What do you think Chuckleberry wants?
Do you think Dad enjoys waking up to Chuckleberry's wet slurp?   Why?

"Good morning," a cheery voice called from above.
It was Mom, greeting her husband with love.
"It's time to get up. It's a beautiful day!
Let's get our three children along on their way."

Dad said, "The plans for the building I designed
Are due to my boss at quarter past nine."
"Well, UP, then," said Mom, and the dog, HE sat up!
"Not you, silly hound dog!" she said to the pup.

Why did Dad have to hurry?
Why did Chuckleberry sit up?

The brown spotted dog let out with a yelp,
And Dad said, "I'm coming to give you some help."
Mom said, "Okay, you can cook up the eggs."
Then Chuck followed Mom, running on his short legs.

In Eric and Brent's room, she called, "C'mon boys!"
But they wouldn't wake up to such little noise.
From under the covers of the two bunk beds
Peeked the tousled hair of their two sleepy heads.

What would be a good way to wake up Eric and Brent?

"You sleepyheads," Mom called, "you'll be late for school!
Being on time is an important rule."
"RARF RARF!" added Chuck, with his tail a-wagging,
And on to Emily's room he went, his long ears a-dragging.

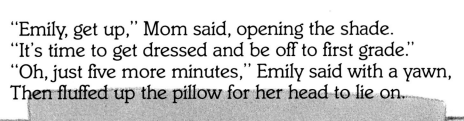

"Emily, get up," Mom said, opening the shade.
"It's time to get dressed and be off to first grade."
"Oh, just five more minutes," Emily said with a yawn,
Then fluffed up the pillow for her head to lie on.

What will happen if Emily falls back to sleep?

"Well, if all they want, Chuck,
Is to stay in bed,
I guess I'll serve YOU
Eggs and pancakes instead!"

But the smell of bacon brought through the door
Eric, Brent, Emily, and Dad—that made four!
Dad took the eggs and cracked open the shells,
And soon the eggs sizzled their own special smells.

Do you like the smell of eggs?   Why?
What other breakfast foods have special smells?
Which breakfast food smells best to you?

"I'm hungry!" cried Eric.   "Eggs sunny side up!"
"Whoa, slow down!" said Dad, taking his cup.
"There seems to be something you all have forgotten."
"I mean *Please!*" Eric said.   "Gosh, my manners are rotten."

What is Eric talking about when he wants his eggs "sunny side up"?
What do you think Eric and the other kids have forgotten?

"That's not it," said Dad to his ten year old son;
To Brent and to Emily, "There are chores to be done."
"I poured the milk Tuesday," Emily chimed in.
"Her job is easy, 'cause she's the youngest," Brent grinned.

"I fed the dog yesterday," Eric complained,
"And walked him outside, though it rained and it rained."
"You must find a way, kids, to work this all out,"
Said Dad, but the children had started to shout.

TIME

What could Dad do if the kids keep arguing about their work?

The kids were all yelling at once, more and more,
And never heard Mr. Stokes knock at their door.
Their kindly old neighbor came in when invited,
And, waving a paper, was very excited.

Will yelling help the kids work out their problem?
What else could they do?
What could Mr. Stokes be excited about?

"Good news, folks!   I won and I owe it to you!"
He said to Brent, Eric, and Emily, too.
"I guessed the right number of nails in the jar
In the hardware store contest.   I was closest by far!"

"You three children, Eric and Emily and Brent,
Are ten, six, and eight, and that's just how it went.
Yes, 1068 was the closest by far
To the number of nails that were in that big jar!"

What other numbers could Mr. Stokes have guessed using the kids' ages?

Dad said, "Shake!" and held out his hand,
But their funny hound dog did not understand.
He held up his paw and was ready to shake.
"I meant Mr. Stokes, Chuck,...For goodness' sake!"

Then Mr. Stokes said, "I think you'll agree,
A big pizza party is just what we need.
That way, I can share my prize winnings with you."
And all the kids answered with one big "YAHOO!"

Do you think the kids have forgotten about their problem?   Why?

Emily said, "This sounds like a fun game,
But what will we do if we all roll the same?"
"No problem," said Eric, "because if we tie,
We'll roll over again for one more try."

What will the kids do if they tie the second time they throw the dice?
What could they use if they didn't have dice?

When Chuck heard "ROLL OVER," then down on the floor
He barked and rolled over, and over some more.
And then he kept barking, from deep in his throat.
Mom said, "Looks like Chuck has just cast his vote!"

The children all shouted, "We DO like that plan!"
That's how their "Chore Choosing Game" all began.
They even thought up a job for their pup—
When breakfast is done, he eats leftovers up!

Do you think Chuckleberry likes his job?   Why?
Does Chuckleberry's job seem hard?   Why?

Now the kids all know their jobs and the rule.
In no time, they're up getting ready for school.
Before you can count, "one, two, three, four,"
Their jobs are all done and they're out of the door!

Think 'n' Tell

How do you like to wake up in the morning?

Would you like a pet like Chuckleberry? Why?

Pretend you are Chuckleberry. How will you wake up someone in our family?

What other ways can you think of to pick jobs at home? Which is the best way? Why?

Should Mom and Dad do all the jobs themselves? Why?

Hilarious Chuckleberry

Chuckleberry does lots of funny tricks in the story. You can make your own Chuckleberry puppet to do the tricks the next time you read *Wakin' to the Bacon.*

What you need:

old sock	scissors
glue	markers
paper bag	buttons
scraps of red and brown fabric	

What to do:

Draw Chuckleberry's face on the bottom of the sock. Or, if you'd like, glue or sew buttons on the sock for his eyes and nose, and yarn for his whiskers.

Next, cut a tongue out of red material. Glue or sew the tongue on the underside of the sock. Be sure the tongue shows when you curl your hand inside the sock.

Don't forget Chuckleberry's long, floppy ears! Cut two ears out of fabric and glue or sew them on the sock. Or, cut Chuck's ears out of the paper bag and glue them on the sock.

Decorate the rest of the bag with a collar, brown spots, or anything else you'd like.

Make Chuckleberry come alive! Put your hand inside the sock so your hand and fingers are Chuckleberry's head. Move your fingers to nod Chuckleberry's head. Next time you read *Wakin' to the Bacon,* pretend that your puppet is Chuck and make him do his tricks.

What other puppets could you make out of these materials?

Breakfast Plate

Wouldn't it be fun to always have what you want for breakfast? Follow these directions to make your own breakfast plate to enjoy over and over again!

What you need: paper plate   crayons   scissors
                     magazine   glue

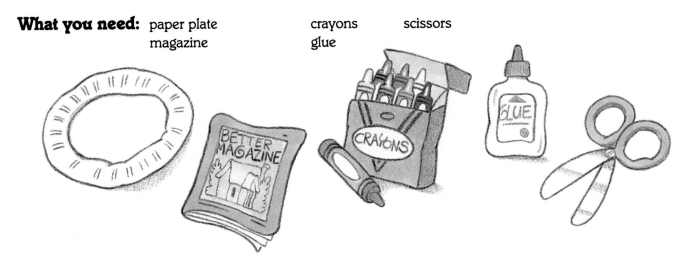

What to do:

Decide what foods you'd like for breakfast.

Use your crayons to draw your breakfast on the paper plate, or cut pictures of food out of magazines and glue them on the plate.

Make some other breakfast plates for your friends. Keep the plates so you can have your friends over for breakfast any time! And best of all—no one has to wash the dishes!

Munch away! But don't eat the plate!

What other things could you make with paper plates? Why don't we use paper plates every day instead of dishes?

Guess How Many

Mr. Stokes won the hardware store contest by guessing the correct number of nails in the jar. Wouldn't it be fun to have your own contest?

What you need:

shoebox	tape
construction paper	scissors
small jar	pencil
small pieces of paper	
small items to fill the jars	
(safety pins, cotton balls, buttons, M&M's or peanuts)	

What to do:

1.

Cover your shoebox with construction paper. Use the scissors to cut a slit in the top of the box, or ask your parent to help.

3. Next, have your friends or members of your family guess how many items are in the jar. Ask them to write their guesses and their names on the small pieces of paper and put them in the covered shoebox.

2. Fill the jar with small items.

4. WINNER!

When everyone has had a chance to guess, count the items in the jar. Look through the papers and announce the winner!

Hold other contests with different items. Were any of the items easier to guess than others? Which ones were easier? Why do you think these items were easier? What would be a good prize for the winning guesser?

Early in the Morning

It's early in the morning,
I hear my sister tell
She took a spelling test
and she did it really well.
She took a spelling test
and she did it really well.
It's early in the morning,
I hear my sister tell.

It's early in the morning,
I hear my brother shout,
"The toothpaste is all gone
and I can't get any out.
The toothpaste is all gone
and I can't get any out."
It's early in the morning,
I hear my brother shout.